**Peter Rimmer** is a photographer and writer based in the North-West of England. Born in Southport, Peter now lives in Wigan. He was awarded a Master's Degree in Photography from the University of Bolton.

*The tide's the very devil* tells a story of shrimp fishermen in Morecambe Bay. The title is taken from the first line of the chorus of a folk song *On Morecambe Bay* written by an old school-friend from Southport. Kevin Littlewood was inspired to write the lyrics following the tragedy in 2004 when 23 Chinese cockle pickers died after becoming trapped by rising tides.

ISBN 978 1 62847 048 2
Publisher: Peter Rimmer (www.photopr.eu)
Photographs: Peter Rimmer
Design: Graham Schofield
Print: Panda Press (Stone) Ltd

# On Morecambe Bay

*For the tide's the very devil,*
*It can run you out of breath,*
*It can race you on the level,*
*It can chase you to your death.*
*Yes the tide's the very devil,*
*And the devil has his day,*
*On the weary cockle grounds of Morecambe Bay.*

# *The tide's the very devil*

### Morecambe Bay in photographs

## Peter Rimmer

# Morecambe Bay

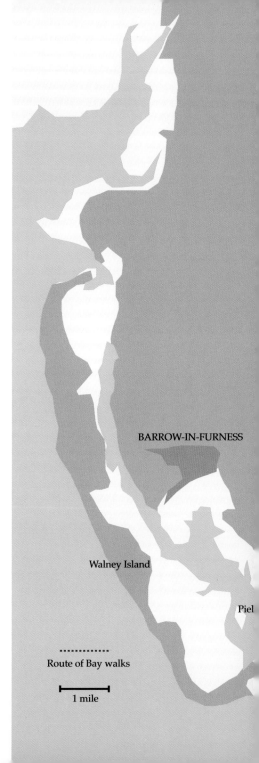

**MORECAMBE BAY** remains one of the last wildernesses in England. A sand plain of one hundred and twenty square miles and more is revealed twice each day by the ebb and flow which carves the sands into subtly different reliefs with each tide. Channels and quicksand come and go, shifting overnight after lying dormant for decades. The shore margins ebb and flow too; grassy marsh is eroded in one place as new land builds up elsewhere.

BARROW-IN-FURNESS

Walney Island

Piel

··············
**Route of Bay walks**

⊢━⊣
1 mile

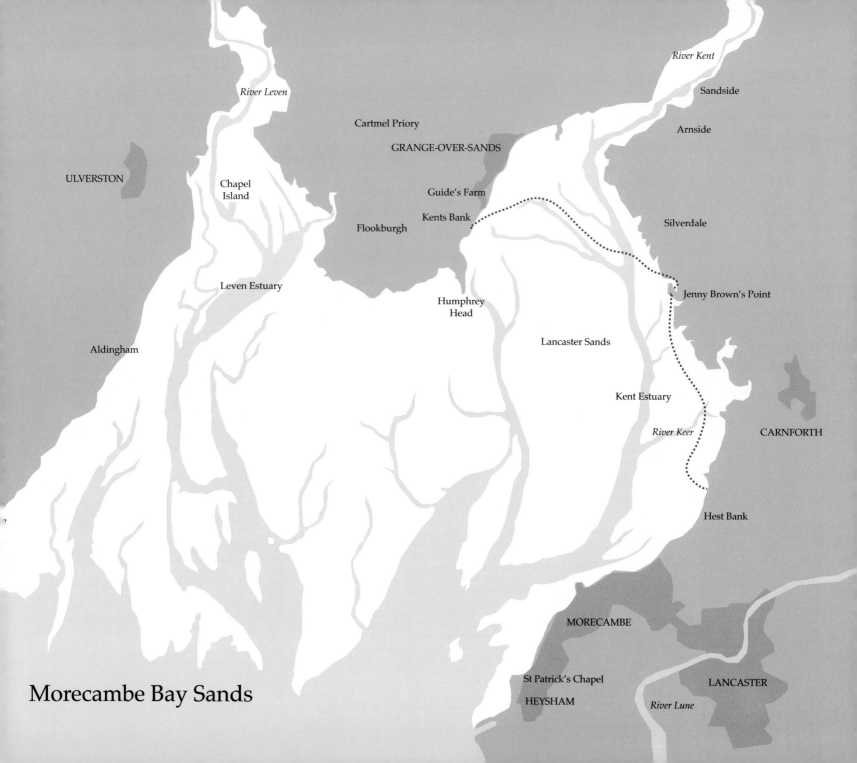

# Morecambe Bay Sands

*River Leven*

*River Kent*

Sandside

Cartmel Priory

Arnside

GRANGE-OVER-SANDS

ULVERSTON

Chapel
Island

Guide's Farm

Silverdale

Kents Bank

Flookburgh

Leven Estuary

Jenny Brown's Point

Humphrey
Head

Lancaster Sands

Aldingham

Kent Estuary

CARNFORTH

*River Keer*

Hest Bank

MORECAMBE

St Patrick's Chapel

LANCASTER

HEYSHAM

*River Lune*

# Walney Island

**WALNEY ISLAND** is a narrow strip of land, eleven miles long, on the western edge of Morecambe Bay. The island is well known for its two extensive coastal nature reserves which are home to a great many species of birds. Walney is connected to the town of Barrow-in-Furness by the Jubilee Bridge, built in 1908.

# Piel Island and Piel Castle

**PIEL ISLAND** has a long and interesting history because of its links to Furness Abbey. The surviving 14th century motte and bailey 'castle' was used as a fortified warehouse to keep cargoes, especially wool, safe from pirates and other raiders. In the early 19th century Piel remained important for shipping entering the harbour and was home to a number of pilots. Piel Castle is managed by English Heritage.

**'Peele Castle in a Storm'** 1805 (oil on canvas), Beaumont, Sir George Howland (1753-1827)
© *Copyright* Leicester Arts & Museums / The Bridgeman Art Library

# Elegiac Stanzas

William Wordsworth
Suggested by a picture of 'Peele Castle in a Storm', painted by Sir George Beaumont

*I was thy neighbour once, thou rugged Pile!*
*Four summer weeks I dwelt in sight of thee:*
*I saw thee every day; and all the while*
*Thy Form was sleeping on a glassy sea.*

*Then, Beaumont, Friend! who would have been the Friend,*
*If he had lived, of Him whom I deplore,*
*This work of thine I blame not, but commend;*
*This sea in anger, and that dismal shore.*

*And this huge Castle, standing here sublime,*
*I love to see the look with which it braves,*
*Cased in the unfeeling armour of old time,*
*The lightning, the fierce wind, and trampling waves.*

*Note*: In 1794 Wordsworth spent part of a summer vacation at the house of his cousin, Mr. Barker, at Rampside, a village near Peele Castle.

**RAMPSIDE** lighthouse is an unpainted tower built with red and light yellow bricks, giving at a distance the appearance of vertical red and white stripes (one white stripe on each of the four faces).

Known locally as 'The Needle', it is the only survivor of 13 range lights built on the approaches to Rampside and Barrow in the period between 1850 and 1870 to aid navigation. It was saved after Rampside residents worked to have it listed as a historic structure.

# The Leven Estuary
# and Chapel Island

**CHAPEL ISLAND** is a limestone outcrop that lies in the Leven Estuary, less than one mile from the shore. The island is on the over-sands route between Ulverston and Lancaster, and accessible at low tide with the help of Ray Porter, the Queen's Guide to the Sands across the Leven Estuary (page 23).

# *Flookburgh*

**FLOOKBURGH** is one of the few towns in England reputedly named after a fish. Most sources think the town takes its name from the 'flukes' – flat fish found in abundance in the bay – but an alternative theory claims that the town was a Norse settlement named after a chieftain called Floki – the old name for the town was Flokeburg.

**FLOOKBURGH FISHERMEN** harvest shrimps by negotiating tides, channels and sinking sand. The small brown shrimp of Morecambe Bay is considered a delicacy due to its unique flavour and texture. The shrimp were first gathered by pushing hand nets on a long pole into the sand. Then horsepower replaced manpower and the horses pulling carts with shrimp nets fastened to them. Today, tractors with trailers are used to rake in the shrimp. After being boiled and picked, most are sold from houses in the village or at Barrow Market.

Jack Butler - c1960

John Wilson - 2012

Ted Wilson - c1960

Michael Wilson - 2012

38

Ted Wilson - c1960

John Wilson - 2012

SHRIMPS are grey when they are alive. After taking out the shells, seaweed, flukes, weaver fish and other debris, the shrimps are boiled up until they turn bright pink. They are then laid out to cool, before being divided up for picking. The same process has been operating for generations.

1960s

2012

Picking shrimps 1972

Picking shrimps 2012

**PLAICE** are an added bonus to the shrimp catch. Caught up in the trawl nets, the small ones are thrown back into the water but the large fish are popular with locals and sold on Barrow Market or from the house.

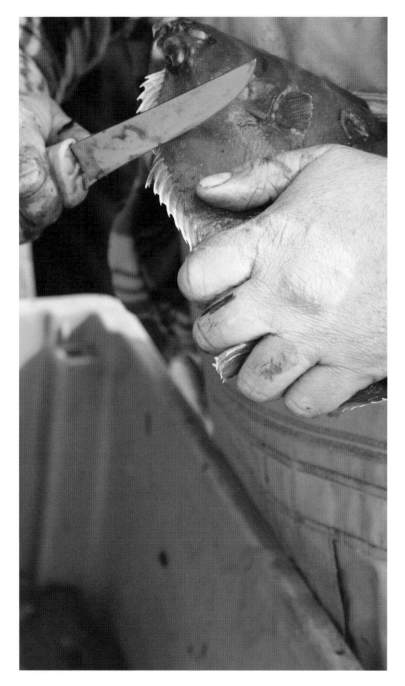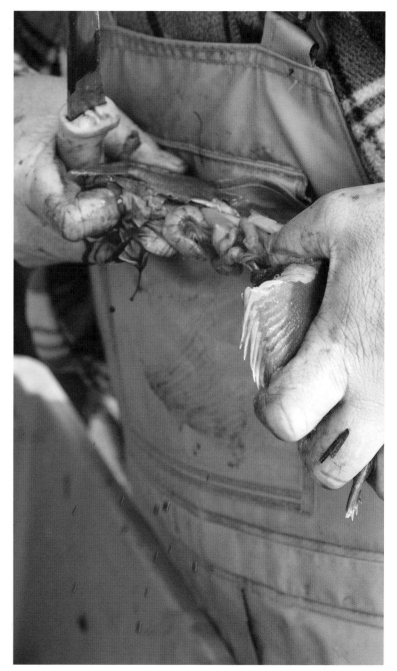

# Humphrey Head

**HUMPHREY HEAD** is a prominent grassed limestone outcrop to the west of Grange-over-Sands and is said to be the place where the last wild wolf in England was shot. It offers panoramic views of Morecambe Bay, and is the destination for some of the Cross Bay Walks.

# The Kent Estuary

**THE RIVER KENT** is a short, fast-flowing river of some 20 miles which runs into the north of Morecambe Bay at Arnside. The deep channel is shown at low tide running close to Sandside Quarry (page 68), and alongside the exposed sands with its channels and 'Loom-holes', deep water-filled holes, which pose a hazard to fishermen and others (page 69).

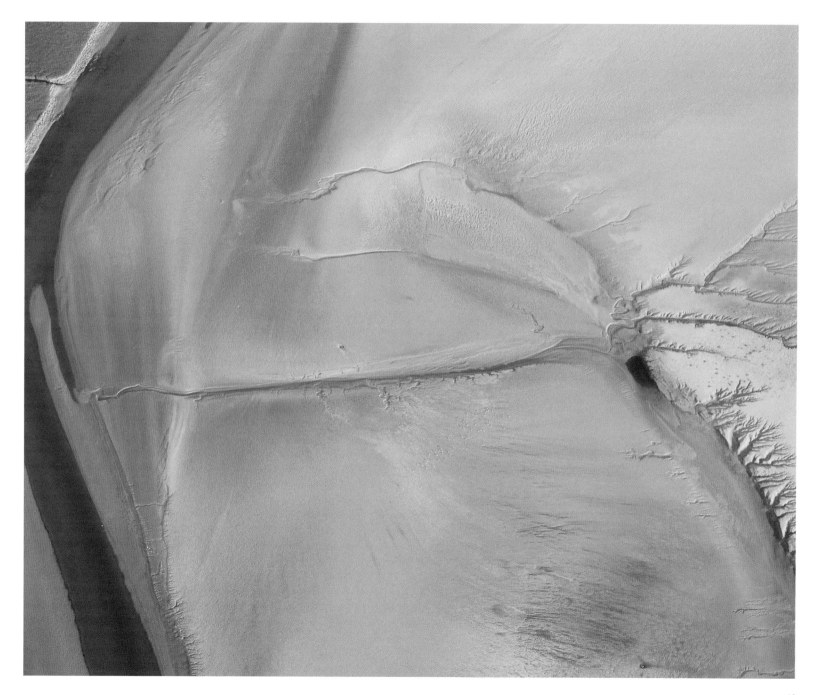

# Crossing Lancaster Sands

**LANCASTER SANDS** has been used for centuries as a quick way to reach the Furness Peninsula from North Lancashire. The route has two sections: the first from the east shore of the bay to Kents Bank and the second across the Leven Sands, past Chapel Island, to Ulverston. Until the building of the railway in 1857 everything travelled this route: goods, prisoners, preachers, poets and painters. Many people died, either drowned or caught in the quicksand, because they did not wait for the guide.

'**Crossing Lancaster Sands**' c1834 (oil on canvas), David Cox the Elder
© *Copyright* Manchester Art Gallery

**CROSS BAY WALKS** are led by Cedric Robinson MBE, the Queen's Official Guide. More than forty guided walks across Morecambe Bay were scheduled for 2012. Many cross the sands between Arnside and Kents Bank.

Bay walks are also led by Alan Sledmore, mainly from Silverdale to Grange-over-Sands or Flookburgh.

As well as the ever-shifting channels, there is also the danger of quicksand.

**THE QUEEN'S GUIDE,**
Cedric Robinson, has been in post for fifty years and is the latest in a long line of 'Sand Pilots' dating back to the 14th century and the Cistercian Monks who arrived in the North-West of England and began the construction of Furness Abbey in 1127. The first guide was appointed in 1536 to take people safely across the Bay.

**BROBS** mark the safe route across the sands. Cedric Robinson uses laurel branches cut from his garden. Known as 'brobs', the visible leaves remain attached despite the salt water.

The 'Office of the Carter' was to go on his white horse (the better to be seen in the mist and semi-darkness) to the river channel as soon as the tide had ebbed. He stuck birch branches or pieces of broom deeply into the sand with the tops exposed to mark his trail.

**THE BAY SEARCH AND RESCUE TEAM** has its primary base at a purpose-built station at Flookburgh. A team of unpaid volunteers combine specialist training with local knowledge to provide support for HM Coastguard, Mountain Rescue Teams and other emergency services on and around Morecambe Bay.

# Cockle picking

COCKLE PICKING in Morecambe Bay was closed in September 2011 and remained closed throughout 2012. The beds were unlikely to re-open in 2013 because there were no known commercial stocks of cockles in Morecambe Bay.

The only cockling in the North-West of England in 2012 took place on the Ribble Estuary at Foulnaze which attracted cocklers from as far afield as Scotland, north and south Wales, and the North-East of England. Stocks throughout the Ribble Estuary cockle beds were at a low level. Approximately 800 tons of cockles were harvested in three weeks from 1 August 2012 exceeding the catch limit of 750 tons; cockle fishery in the Ribble was closed until further notice.

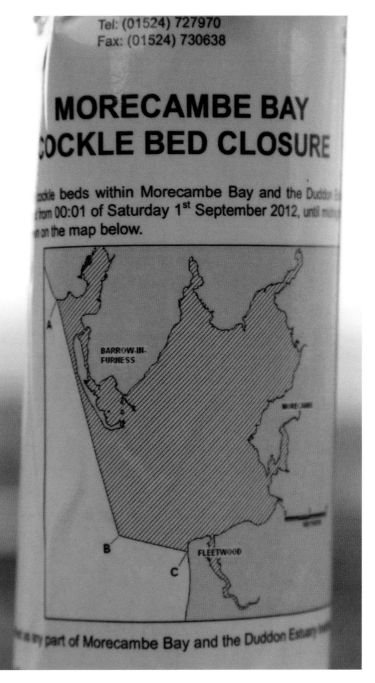

**Tel: (01524) 727970**
**Fax: (01524) 730638**

# MORECAMBE BAY
# COCKLE BED CLOSURE

ockle beds within Morecambe Bay and the Duddon
from 00:01 of Saturday 1st September 2012, until
on the map below.

BARROW-IN-FURNESS

A

B

C

FLEETWOOD

part of Morecambe Bay and the Duddon Estuary

Cockle pickers at Grange-over-Sands, February 1916

# Old Heysham

**OLD HEYSHAM** is a small fishing village due east of Walney Island with cottages dating back to the 1600s. Overlooked by St Patrick's Chapel, built in Saxon times (600-800 AD), the peace and tranquillity is captured by John D Fox of Bingley, echoing the style of William McGonagall, Bard of Dundee:

*Heysham – thou sweet retreat. Haven of rest.*
*We love thee very much, if not the best.*
*We love thy grand old church, thy rocky shore,*
*Where lovers plight their troth for evermore.*

# ...yes the tide's the very devil

**THE SANDS** have claimed the lives of hundreds of people over the centuries; fishermen, travellers and cockle pickers have all fallen victim to the dangerous tides, quicksands and deep channels.

On 7 November 1912, two brothers and their cousin were drowned as a violent storm raged. Francis Robinson (21) and his cousins Edward (32) and Thomas (30) made for home in the darkness but missed the angle of the channel and ran aground on a sandbank. Francis' body was found due west of Aldingham church; an hour later Edward was washed up. The third body was washed ashore a year later. Flookburgh Church was packed with 500 mourners for the funeral of Francis and Edward.

One of the first recorded deaths was of Michael de Furness who drowned on his return to Aldingham in 1269.

In February 2004, 23 Chinese cockle pickers died after becoming trapped by rising tides near Hest Bank.

EX... AT FLOOKBURGH OF TWO OF THE MORECAMBE BAY VICTIMS NOV: 11th 1912

## ...and the devil has his day

**CARTMEL PRIORY** has a graveslab dedicated to Robert Harrison, who drowned in 1782 aged 23, and to his mother Margaret Harrison who was drowned in the same place almost a year later aged 48.

# Acknowledgements

My special thanks and gratitude go to John Wilson, Flookburgh fisherman, and his son Michael, for their support, kindness and friendship. Without their help this book would not have been possible. Thanks also to their wives, June Wilson and Sharon Wilson, for making me feel like one of the family, and to my partner Sandie Brown and my son Robert for their support and encouragement.

My thanks also to:

Ian Beesley and Terry Speake, the University of Bolton
Jackie Fay, Kendal Library
Peter Harrison, Southport fisherman
Colin Hodgson and the Bay Search and Rescue Team
Kate Holliday at the Cumbria Archive Centre in Kendal
Kevin Littlewood, singer and songwriter of Southport
Jack Manning of Flookburgh
Martin Orrom of Kendal
Ray Porter, the Queen's Guide to the Leven Sands
Cedric Robinson, the Queen's Guide to the Kent Sands
Peter Wade, Morecambe Bay guided walks
Bridgeman Art Library
Manchester Museum/Whitworth Art Gallery